THE CLIMBING MI

STOP NAIL BITING.
IN LESS THAN 66 DAYS. FOR A LIFETIME.

By Oliver Scholz

TABLE OF CONTENTS

Prologue

Prelude

First of all, I would like to thank you for the confidence you have shown in me. You have actively decided to solve a problem and I will accompany you for the next weeks. I'll help you build a new attitude to life. We achieve this with visually appealing hands and, above all, a new self-confidence. Well-groomed fingers are not a utopian notion, you will get closer to this ideal every day and the successes will give you further impetus. You will never lose sight of the goal. Nail biting will undoubtedly accompany you for a long time and you will have tried to stop it. But from now on it will not only be a trial. Results will follow and with new self-confidence you will go into a well-groomed and visually appealing future.

Your body is your friend

Nails grow on average 0.1 millimeters per day or three millimeters per month. Fingernails grow faster than toenails and the middle finger grows faster than thumbs. But let's not get lost in the details. It is important to know that the body is an ally in the fight against chewing. He's making your nails grow permanently. It is therefore unfair if we let him down and simply "bite off" the progress.

A field report

I myself can no longer remember why I started biting. But one thing is certain: it started in my childhood. This has been throughout my entire school career, apprenticeship and parts of my studies. But someday I had enough of it and came up with a method that even allowed me to stop biting. I was often nervous, especially when it came to concentration tasks such as homework. I used my nails as compensation for the inner restlessness. This does not have to be the case and it has negative consequences without exception. Of course, everyone is aware of this, but you can't turn it off without further ado. You're gonna know this.

Chapter 1 - The phenomen of biting nails

Obsession
An obsession describes the compulsive notion that influences a person's actions. When it comes to nail biting, this is clearly a negative obsession. By definition, however, these obsessions are not always negative. In sports or other hobbies, a small portion of ambition is recommended to achieve goals and maintain motivation.

OCD
A more specific categorisation of biting would be that of obsessive-compulsive disorder. This is called OCD and describes an inner compulsion to think or do certain things. The people affected know of their problem, sometimes fight against it, but they can't show any strength of will or see the fight against it as pointless. Older names for this are obsessive-compulsive neuroses. But no matter how you want to divide up biting, it is a mild mental disorder and you should first of all acknowledge this. Insight is the first way to recovery (take this phrase not angry at the place).

Onychophagia

The medical term for nail biting is called onychophagia in expert circles. This disease also appears in the International Statistical Classification of Diseases and Related Health Problems (ICD). The exact classification is given by the cryptic designations F 98.8 and F 98.81: behavioural and emotional disorders with the beginning of childhood and adolescence. Other known disorders fall into this category: nose drilling, thumb sucking and stuttering.

This diagnosis may sound harsh at first, and maybe it'll shock you too. But knowledge of a medical term can also have positive effects. On the one hand, you accept your situation better because you are not alone with a problem and on the other hand you know that there is a realistic chance of reaching the goal.

Enough of grey theory, though. We now want to get into the topic and understand how to put a negative routine behind it, and we want to do it permanently! The great advantage of the method presented later will be that it can be used for all similar problems, not only for nail biting. It is important to understand, analyse and counteract the mechanisms behind the actions.

Chapter 2 – The psyche of mankind

Maxwell Maltz

I would like to dedicate this chapter to a gentleman who has been involved in behavioural research for some time. Mr. Maltz was born in 1889 in New York City and was a plastic surgeon by profession. In this activity, he noted that it takes an average of 21 days for people to cope with a new situation. Be it an amputated leg or an operated face, it was always a similar period of time. These experiences led to the publication of the book "Psycho-Cybernetics" in 1960, which is still a bestseller to this day. It's sold over 30 million copies.

Success gurus

This success naturally led to numerous success coaches who adapted these insights to convince people of their methods. It was no longer spoken for at least 21 days, but for exactly 21 days. Elsewhere you can find other numbers, for example 30 or any x-number. But it is precisely these promises that have prevailed, because they are memorable and define a precise goal. There are three reasons for this, in my opinion:

1st   A clear formulation is easy to understand.
2nd   People are inspired by the low number 21
        ("Wow, I can change my whole life in just three weeks!")
3rd   The period does not seem unrealistic, since it takes several weeks. Nevertheless, it is clearly too short.

The problem is that Maltz only used his own perception and didn't conduct any real empirical research. It is, of course, heading in the right direction, but is it really only 21 days at least?

A study on behavioural change

In a study published in the "European Journal of Social Psychology", Philippa Lally and her team from University College London investigated how long it may take to change his habit.

They examined 96 people over a period of twelve weeks. Each participant chose a habit and reported daily whether it was observed or not.
At the end of the twelve weeks, the researchers investigated how long it took each person to automate the respective activity.

The result of the study was that it took an average of more than two months for a habit to automatically expire. More precisely, it was 66 days on average. But here too, however, we can only point to the average. There are people who implement adaptions slower (254 days) and others who have been able to implement a fixed routine in their lives after only 18 days.

Does only 100% compliance lead to the goal?
The study aimed to show that 95% of the respondents adhered to their new habits. This leads to the assumption that there had to be individual days when the targets were not met. It won't be a big step backwards if you don't reach the day's goal. But if two or three days creep in, when you lose sight of the target, you don't have to be careful not to lose any momentum. Momentum describes the impulse that characterizes the mechanical state of movement of a physical object. This could be imagined using a coal-powered locomotive. The locomotive only gets into operation slowly at the beginning, as the enormous weight prevents a fast start. In addition, a certain amount of energy has to be used to move the transmissions and finally the axles with the wheels. Once the locomotive has picked up speed for some time, it is almost impossible to stop. This can be compared to nail biting. You are on day 17 and you've only had two days of biting so far. Nevertheless, the momentum prevents you from ruining your complete success on a single day, as you can already feel and see the success you have achieved so far.

The path is the goal
As you've noticed so far, getting used to bad habits is no easy task. It is sometimes associated with hard work. Therefore, you should start

to put the system into action as soon as possible. Mark a start date in the calendar and make all necessary preparations. You will experience these preparations in the course of the book. With the example of the momentum, you will also have realized that the accustoming is not a 100 meter run. It is rather a marathon, with comparatively slow steps, but steady.

At this point I would like to praise you once again: you have already achieved more than you are likely to notice. You first realized that it was bad to bite nails, then you found out about solutions on the internet and you came across my method. Last but not least, you have read the book up to this point and haven't lost your courage. Respect for this and many thanks for the trust! This means that you have already completed just under five of the 42 kilometres. Many people are constantly reading new knowledge, but will never become theoretical experts. This won't happen to you, you're already too far advanced   for   that!

Chapter 3 - Biting and the consequences

Why does nail biting bother you at all?

Does it have any value at all to think about the question? Isn't biting a habit that should be rejected from the ground up, such as drinking milk straight from the pack in the refrigerator and then putting it back in the fridge, or constantly pulling out the smartphone at private meetings? I think that everyone is aware of his or her actions, but it doesn't hurt to focus even more on this. When you look at the exact consequences, you see the urgency again and develop an improved focus on the negative habit. To try to stop them then goes much deeper into one's own psyche and one develops a thirst for action, which was not even present in the beginning.

Physical follow

We are all aware that nail biting has very negative obvious effects. Truncated nails are a figurehead and look like a business card. Inflammation and damaged nails and fingertips are known symptoms of biting. Poorly groomed hands can affect a complete outfit of an otherwise attractive person. Whether with a gala dress or a fancy suit, bitten nails simply don't fit into the picture. But apart from the purely optical reasons, there are also other consequences for the body that one might not suspect at first glance.

My parents always encouraged me to wash my hands when I enter my own house. We take in innumerable bacteria, whether in the subway, on the shopping trolley or during small talk with a colleague. A handshake can suffice to infect you with a flu. And that's exactly where the problem lies, because let's face it: you can't wash your hands often enough to protect yourself from these dangers. Of course, bacteria can be absorbed without biting, for example by coughing or sneezing, but by nibbling you expose yourself to a much greater risk. I myself often had the feeling that this negative habit led to at least a slight cold being the result.

Do they keep in mind again and again when they become weak again: is it really worthwhile to devalue themselves visually and then endanger their health?

Mental follow
In addition to the physical consequences, psychic ones play an equally important role. A comparison would be with a smoker. I have to say that I've been and will probably be smoke-free all my life, because who starts smoking at the end of my 20s? Nevertheless, I have often been unable to see the parallels. I have always wondered how people can do this to their bodies and why they don't stop doing it. But when I wanted to stop biting every now and then, I noticed how hard it is to throw such a vice. But it is identical from the psychological pressure: one wants to stop absolutely, but it lacks the will power to pull it through and this leads to the fact that one feels all the weaker, if one cannot bring it to an end then again once again.

You know very well that you are nervous and out of control at the moment of weakness, you lose supremacy over your behaviour and this is an enormous psychological pressure that you can literally feel on your shoulders.

Self-confidence is increasingly being scratched in this aspect and a small vicious circle of disgust and dependency begins. The vice becomes a part of life that one would most like to shake off, but it seems to be overpowering.

The external impact
Another important point is the external impact. How does nail biting affect other people? I have always had concerns about my fingers being misjudged by other people or being approached about the nails. Let's face it: a romantic date with your favourite Italian, she or

he takes your hand, the candlelight caresses your hands and then the other person looks more closely at your fingers. This can be a no-go, especially because women are known to look after well-groomed hands. The first impression is often decisive and if you can't score points in body care, the chances of success are even worse.

But also in the family, one is often asked about it, especially because they are more directly confronted with criticism than in the wider circle of acquaintances. The parents and grandparents are to be particularly emphasized here, because they only want your best and want to inspire you to rethink. This is still unpleasant and will not stop until you have left the truck. The same goes for finding a partner, but that's another matter.

Another field is the professional. Bitten nails don't make a good impression in an interview. If you can't hide them skillfully, the personeler inevitably thinks about the negative qualities that are associated with them. He could associate that one is unbalanced and it is interpreted as a weakness of character. It may also be the case with regard to possible promotion, that for this reason one is not taken into consideration, since it seems that one is all the more overtaxed with more responsibility and this is reflected in the psychological consequences.

Chapter 4 – Know the triggers

Trigger finder

So far we have talked a lot about general information and the consequences of nail biting, but why and in what situation do you get caught up in your obsession? You can only change your behaviour if you know in which situations you are vulnerable. In the following chapter I describe the most important sensations that lead to nail biting. Read this carefully and ask yourself after each subitem whether this is true for you. It has proven to be particularly useful to record these moments in a list. Writing things down has the effect that you are more aware of it and it is also clearer in your thoughts. If you have never thought about your behaviour pattern before, it makes sense to create a list in advance. You can always write down places, moments and feelings where you have become weak. This means that you can classify yourself in the categories and take the appropriate precautions. It is recommended to create this list as soon as possible before starting the program. This doesn't take away your motivation because you started the procedure unprepared.

Type: stress

Stress refers to the psychological and physical stress of a person in situations of special demands. These requirements can vary in nature. Some people feel stress when they enter a narrow elevator, others feel stress when they do difficult homework at school. If one has a high resistance to stress, symptoms of combating symptoms occur much later than in sensitive persons. In the end, however, no one is immune to stress, it may only occur later. In the course of this book we will of course focus on stress control by nail biting. As already explained in the section Trigger-Finder you should be aware of which situations lead to stress. This may sound banal in some cases, but it should be noted down. Once you have grasped the situations, you can see below whether you are represented in the Stress Type category. This helps to limit the situations that could potentially pose a risk of going to the nails or skin.

Type: boredom

The boredom guy is from the circle of people who get nervous when they are not active and look for work. There is a lack of satisfaction in the hands, one would prefer to use it, but one has nothing to do. This behavior pattern therefore often leads to biting. Often you are also lost in thoughts, so that you only catch yourself biting relatively late. This group of people is helped by an activity that can be carried out by hand. There are constructive and destructive possibilities. Learning a musical instrument, painting or juggling with a pen would be constructive. Smoking cigarettes would be destructive, because you exchange one truck for another. In the next chapter, we will again talk about possibilities which are a suitable distraction.

Type: social anxiety

The people who belong to this group are mostly shy people who find it difficult to deal with others. They bite in the presence of other people, mainly those who feel the greatest insecurity. This can be in the circle of colleagues or at school. This group feels inferior and has a social phobia to enjoy the company of others or just to endure. It is important to learn to get along with other people and to get along with them. This may sound very simple, but social phobias can be managed. It is doubtful whether nail biting is the biggest and primary problem. A conversation with a therapist, family or friends could provide clarity. If you belong to this group of people, I recommend that you consult an expert's guide. A few years ago, I myself benefited greatly from a guide on the female gender, because often misconceptions are manifested in the train of thought, whether from education or the environment.

It should be noted that introversion is no problem. Introverted people, unlike extroverted people, don't seem so open, but they are psychologically stable and have a healthy self-confidence. If you are extremely shy, however, this is definitely the problem that should be tackled first.

Type: perfectionism

Congratulations! I think you belong to the group that can best announce the fight to its vice. Perfectionists are people who want to see a small mistake in their fingernails every now and then and want to eliminate it on the spot. You often notice that biting is not the right way to get a well-formed nail, but you lose yourself in a vicious circle of improvements. They don't manage to leave the descent five straight and wait for the evening at home, where you can calmly straighten the one corner with the file.

Experience has shown that the people of the perfectionists are the easiest way to stop biting. This is because there are fewer situations where you can bite as nails are growing. On the other hand, biting is not so much anchored subconsciously, since one only wants to improve the appearance.

Type: confrontation

Members of this association have the problem that they are not able to deal well with verbal confrontations. They are sensitive in type and often have problems with their stomach or nails. But being sensitive is no problem, on the contrary! One is usually more empathetic and is perceived as honest by other people. However, unpleasant conversations with colleagues or friends lead to a loss of control and the start of biting. They cannot deal with angry people and criticism (constructive as well as destructive) does not roll off easily.

Note: It is very likely that one can and will belong to several groups at the same time. I would associate myself with the group stress and boredom. On the one hand, problems led to problems, especially with tasks in studies, but also to boredom that was not fully utilized, which led to nail biting. I have analyzed this before and was able to prepare myself for such situations and knew when I was vulnerable. In these situations, one should rely on mental strength and have the aids presented in the next chapter ready.

Chapter 5 - Self-help help

Many roads lead to Rome
In this chapter I would like to introduce you to some specific procedures that will help you to prevent biting. It is important to note that some more and others will not like you very much. After an unbiased evaluation or a short test phase you can choose the best method. It is up to you whether you use three methods of assistance or just one to support the mountaineering method. Ultimately, what counts is the result of climbing the mountain.

Chewing gum
Experience has shown that biting is rarely or only a little bit when you have chewing gum in your mouth and your teeth are busy. Make sure you always carry a pack with you, especially in situations where you tend to bite. Supporters of chewing gum will be able to use this trick easily. Chewing gum should be used in a targeted way, not just more often. You know the dangerous situations through your analysis and chewing gum is the easiest way to master them.
For people who don't like chewing gum at all, we recommend those with little taste. Sugar should always be avoided. Besides, you can always enjoy a good breath, but please don't smack your lips!

Scissor and file
This technique has proven itself especially with perfectionists. It is best to get a travel set with scissors and file so that you can always carry it comfortably with you. If you find an unpleasant spot in your nails, a short walk to the toilet is enough and you can file your fingers straight again. I don't think it is necessary to mention that filing doesn't go down well with others.

Clear varnish against nail biting
This is a good technique to coat the fingernail with unpleasant taste. When biting, the acidic expression in the mouth is immediately noticeable and stops. There is also clear varnish containing a hardener.

Especially for soft fingernails, it helps to make the fingers more resistant.

The disadvantage is that the clear varnish does not appear to be 100% transparent. You always see a slight gleam and that can be unpleasant for men. The disadvantage is that the clear varnish cannot be applied far away on the skin, so that it cannot be used as compensation.

Artificial nails and manicure

The manicure procedure is especially recommended for women. The decision can be made whether it should be a simple manicure, where the natural nail is cared for and possibly coated with paint, or whether it should be used directly on the wrong nails. Your own style is required. If plastic nails are not liked, this technique should not be used and only varnishes should be used. The disadvantage is that you can easily reach the skin next to the nails without the bitter substances in your mouth. Also the costs should be considered, these can quickly exceed 40 euros, besides, not everyone can become friends with the thought of false fingernails.

Limitation

This is done by concentrating on one nail. There is therefore only one nail to bite on, which makes the cold withdrawal easier. Maybe you already had a certain nail or a hand that you liked before? Then it can help to keep this restriction, but not to go over to other nails if you have already bitten to the end. If you stick to this technique, the nail will eventually hurt a lot as you will go further than usual, because there is no alternative. The pain will help you on your way to Purchasing Life.

Replacement

Another possibility is to look for employment for the hands. As already mentioned, this can be divided into constructive and destructive. An activity that trains you and broadens your horizons should of course be preferred to smoking. Here you can freely develop your creativity. You always wanted to play an instrument or paint? Then start it! You realize that your skills are not sufficient for acceptable painterly results? Then buy a canvas with pre-defined fields or a book explaining the basics. There are no excuses to put a long-awaited wish into practice. In addition, these activities calm you down and allow you to build mental strength, because you can quickly see successes that can be projected on nail biting.

Discussion with family/friends

Talk to people who know your problem. Talk to people who care that you ruin your nails. Tell them that you have made a decision and want to defeat your vice with a new method. This method helps you to communicate your problem and it is better to have shared your feelings with others. In addition, it creates a certain social pressure that gives you a boost. The pressure is like a shadow that accompanies you all the time and reminds you of the successes you have achieved the next time you see someone else. In addition, people can remind you to bite if you are in thoughts and they notice it. They know about your vice and want to help you get past it.

Adapt nutrition

As already mentioned, nails grow about 0.1 millimeters per day depending on the person's finger and age. However, this process can be influenced a little bit. You are what you eat, this also applies to the nails. Calcium, magnesium and omega 3 fatty acids are important nutrients for this purpose, i. e. a healthy and balanced diet.

Another nutrient is biotin, which is particularly responsible for nail growth. You will find it in the following foods: eggs, carrots, cucumbers, tomatoes, lentils, almonds, cauliflower, peanuts and oats (flakes) and nettle tea.

Nutritional supplements are also often mentioned, for example those that supply the biotin separately to the body or similar. These are offered at a high price and often do not have the desired effect. If you feel the need for manicures, it is best to talk to your family doctor or pharmacist or an expert in the field of manicures.

Treatment with household remedies
It has also proved useful to massage in oils. The traditional household remedies are coconut oil, olive oil and linseed oil. At best, you do this before going to bed and put on cotton gloves that you wear overnight.

You can also soak your hands in lemon or orange juice for about 10 minutes. The fruits contain a lot of vitamin C, which strengthens the nails and can accelerate growth.

Chapter 6 – The climbing method

The method briefly explained

Maybe you remember it from your childhood: you have the longed for desire to buy a toy, but the five marks pocket money was not enough to realize this in a short time. For this reason, one of them gave up the wish to save money until he could afford the toy. But beyond that, there were children who were particularly creative and visualized this saving process using a thermometer or graphic. They drew another line for every five marks, which came closer and closer to the target. From this they have learned the motivation to work towards a longer-term goal that cannot be achieved directly. They have invested, accepted a short-term renunciation of consumption and in the end received a big reward.

Why shouldn't this also work with the nails? You work towards a goal in the long term and finally you achieve it. Of course, one has to take into account that the goal is not a material value, but a change of behavior which has manifested itself in the mind.

The Climber

You are the mountaineer in the climbing method. The aim is to get the mountaineer to the top of the mountain. It is advisable to deal openly with this role play. Identifying with the figure has a similar effect to reading a book in the form of an ego or immersing oneself in a fantasy world with an image. The other ego experiences adventure and you can support it from a safe distance. Nevertheless, you get a feeling for this idea over time and you also dive in. We are also taking advantage of this effect. The effort is very low, but the resulting Mindset is priceless. However, since only the imagination alone is not enough, we will take a visual aid at hand.

This system can also be used very well with children. You can tell your child a great story about a mountaineer and he or she can identify with it. Every evening you will check whether the nails have been left alone. This teaches the child to keep track of long-term goals and receive rewards for effort.

The diagram is our playing field

You now know what is behind the method, but now I explain the concrete procedure. We will draw a diagram on a paper in preparation. This will represent the playing field or the mountain. A diagram is the graphic representation of proportions and has two axes. The X axis is horizontal and the Y axis is vertical. Here's an example:

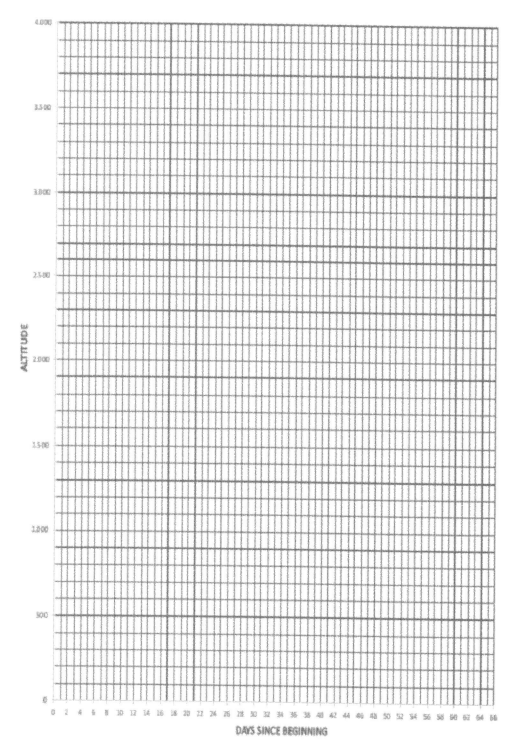

If you've been shocked, don't worry. It won't be mathematical, at least not so bad, that it can stop you from succeeding.

In our case, the X-axis represents the number of days since you implemented this method. I suggest that a total of 66 days should be allowed. This number of days reflects a realistic duration in which you can stop biting.

If you have chosen the chequered DIN A4 paper, the maximum number of possible days is about 60. Set the intersection point of the axes or the zero point almost completely to the left and pull the axis completely to the right. Then you mark the axis: every half centimetre (a box width) reflects a day.

The Y-axis represents the altitude difference. Here it is a little bit more demanding to choose a suitable scaling. With the chequered DIN A4 paper, you can proceed as follows: each half centimetre (one box width) represents 100 height meters. This means that you need five centimeters for 1,000 meters of altitude.

Note: The scaling can be freely selected at your own discretion! If you prefer to work on DIN A3, you can do it with pleasure, here the effec comes across all the more and you motivate yourself a little bit more.

What do you need for the visual field?
You don't need a lot of tools to create the chart:

- a pen
- a ruler
- one sheet of paper

That's it already? Only three items? Yeah, that's right, you read right. We want to approach it according to the KISS system (Keep it simple and stupid - make it as easy as possible).

It can be said that thicker pencils are recommended. By this I mean slightly thicker fine liners, medium thick felt pens or similar. This means that the lines drawn daily are not too thin. Especially with ballpoint pens or pencils it can lead to the effect not being good. The lines don't look strong and motivating, so you should grab something powerful.

The ruler should ideally be 30 centimetres long, as the diagram can then be drawn with a line. I recommend a clean elaboration of the playing field, as this field is looked at daily and the aesthetics play an important role. If you are dissatisfied, make it new!

There are two options for the paper. Either you use squared paper or white printer paper without guide lines. The first one is slightly lighter, the second one is more aesthetic. You can decide for yourself what's more important to you. Basically, the course of the plaid paper and not too thin pencil can also be seen well.

Alternative: if you are fit, you can create this chart yourself in Excel. You can also send an e-mail to "climbingmethod@web.com" and you will receive a print-ready PDF file of the diagram in DIN A4 format.

The traffic light system
The system of a normal traffic light circuit describes the process of "pulling" best. The following definitions apply to the three different colors:

Green: you have mastered today with flying colors. You didn't bite (almost) anything and had yourself under control in every situation! Your preparations have borne fruit, you have anticipated stressful situations and been able to prevent biting in advance. "Fast" means: you were one or two times in thoughts and bit briefly, but you stopped it immediately. Here too, the day can be considered a success! Don't be too hard on yourself and therefore feel free to

approach your new claim appropriately. You can count 100 meters o
altitude difference. Draw a diagonally upward line in the diagram.

Yellow: You have caught yourself biting every now and then, whethe
in your mind or in a stressful situation. You should read through you
preliminary work again and continue to focus on prevention. You are
not allowed to draw in any altitude difference today, but you will no
lose any progress. Therefore, you can draw a horizontal line and
continue working on yourself tomorrow.

Red: You have thrown all the resolutions over the heap and you have
not been able to stop biting. Either you've had a bad day, or you
preliminary work needs to be reworked. Unfortunately, you have to
subtract a few meters of altitude difference from your previous
success. Draw a diagonally downward line into the diagram. Don't le
it get you down, tomorrow the hiking boots will be put on and
attacked again!

You should make your move every day at similar times. Of course it i
advisable to do this before going to bed. This habit will soon find it
way into your rhythm and you won't forget this important ritual.

Reward system
Part of this system is the implementation of rewards. You can choose
these yourself and are completely free to choose. You've been
thinking about an issue for quite some time? How about if this is you
reward for staying up to a certain number of meters of altitude? In the
reward system you can freely unfold, you can define the altitude
difference yourself and the reward as well. This trick will boost you
motivation even more, as you can achieve other goals in parallel
besides defeating your vice of nail-biting.

As an example, you can use the thousands of brands. The first reward
would be reached at 1,000 meters and the second at 2,000 meters
You will see that the number of days between rewards will decrease

This is because you have received the first reward and the motivation is significantly increased.

End of game

The end of this game is at your discretion, but you should not stop before the 66 days indicated. If you have survived these loosely you can dare to do it without the system overcoming everyday life. Some people reach the 3,000 height meters after 40 days, but such persons are of course fit after 20 more days and have reached the goal. If you are still unsure and can see a lot of up and down movements in the diagram, then I recommend you to continue the technique. You can create a new diagram that starts at day 67 and enters the altitude you are at.

In the following I will show you a possible course of your diagram. The horizontal line is a reward:

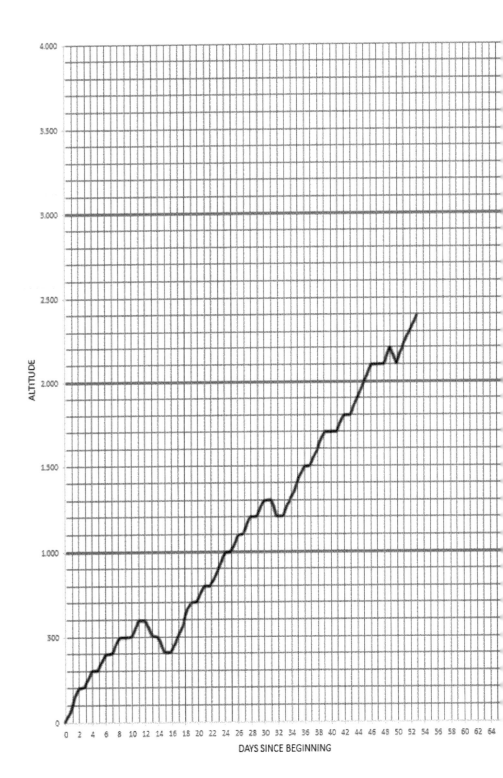

Epilogue

Dealing with setbacks

I know from my own experience that the project often sounds easier than it actually is. But I appeal again to your mental strength! You've shown tremendous commitment. You've read the whole book and you haven't given up changing your life. There will be setbacks every now and then. You're gonna get caught biting and you won't be able to turn it off right away. You may have a cheating day and destroy a lot of success, but this cannot be the end. Motivate yourself every day by continuing to work on your chart. Think of your rewards! Your body is your friend, he will always stand behind you and let all ten fingers work hard for you. Don't let him down and turn your life into a positive one! Probably the most effective method is your own environment. Tell your family and friends about your plans and let them control your success. This pressure to succeed and the newly won Mindset will be a great support for you. Be aware that these new thoughts influence your subconscious so much that your habits are directed into positive paths. Always think positively, even in case of setbacks! Make yourself aware of your past achievements and don't let negative thoughts take over your mind.

My last words

Thank you for reading my Book.and a lot of success! I hope my translation from German is okay. A big thank you goes to DeepL! If you liked reading this adviser I would appreciate an honest amazon review.

Watch your thoughts, for they become words.
Watch your words, for they become actions.
Watch your actions, for they become habits.
Keep your habits in mind, because they will become your character.
Watch your character, for he will become your destiny.
Talmud

Oliver Scholz is represented by:

Marino Scholze
Kronprinzenstraße 57
57250 Netphen
Germany

Printed in Great Britain
by Amazon